AN ARCTIC ECOSYSTEM

Greg Roza

The Rosen Publishing Group's

PowerKids Press™

New York

Published in 2009 by The Rosen Publishing Group, Inc.
29 East 21st Street, New York, NY 10010

Book Design: Daniel Hosek

Photo Credits: Cover © Keenan Ward/Corbis; p. 5 (top) © Ted Spiegel/National Geographic/Getty Images;
pp. 5 (bottom), 12 © Galen Rowell/Corbis; p. 10 © Puku/Grand Tour/Corbis; p. 11 © Andreas Gradin/
Shutterstock; p. 14 © Micha Pawlitzki/zefa/Corbis; p. 15 (top) © George Burba/Shutterstock; p. 15
(bottom left) © Jean-Pierre Lavoie/Shutterstock; p. 15 (bottom right) © TT Photo/Shutterstock; p. 16 © Paul
Nicklen/National Geographic/Getty Images; p. 17 (left) © Dan Guravich/Corbis; p.17 (arctic fox) © Sam
Chadwick/Shutterstock; p. 17 (ground squirrel) © John M. Fugett/Shutterstock; p. 17 (reindeer) © Moodboard/
Corbis; p. 17 (polar bear) © Florida Stock/Shutterstock; p. 18 (butterfly) © Sherry Yates Sowell/Shutterstock;
p. 18 (caterpillar) © Joseph Calve/Shutterstock; p. 18 (grasshopper) © Mitchell Franklin/Shutterstock; p. 18
(beetle) © Masanori Kosugi/Sebun Photo/Getty Images; p. 18 (mosquito) © Richard T. Nowitz/Corbis;
p. 19 © Jack Cronkhite/Shutterstock; p. 20 © Jennifer Stone/Shutterstock; p. 21 (top) © Steve Orsillo/
Shutterstock; p. 21 (bottom) © Robert Pickett/Corbis; p. 22 © Theo Allofs/Corbis; p. 23 © Visuals Unlimited/
Corbis; p. 24 © Dean Conger/Corbis; p. 25 © Macduff Everton/Corbis; p. 26 © Wolfgang Kaehler/Corbis;
p. 27 © Andrew Buckin/Shutterstock; p. 29 © Jan Martin Will/Shutterstock.

Library of Congress Cataloging-in-Publication Data

Roza, Greg.
  An arctic ecosystem / Greg Roza.
    p. cm. — (Real life readers)
  Includes index.
  ISBN: 978-1-4358-0149-3 (paperback)
  6-pack ISBN: 978-1-4358-0150-9
  ISBN 978-1-4358-2983-1 (library binding)
  1. Biotic communities—Arctic regions—Juvenile literature. 2. Ecology—Arctic regions—Juvenile literature.
I. Title.
  QH84.1.R69 2009
  577.0911'3--dc22

                                    2008042718

Manufactured in the United States of America

A VERY COLD PLACE

Do you live where it snows during the winter months, or have you ever visited a place like that? People who live where it gets cold in winter need to protect themselves against the weather. This means dressing warmly when they go outside. If you lived in the Arctic, you'd need to dress warmly for 8 to 9 months out of the year!

The Arctic is the most northern area on Earth. It's made up of the Arctic Ocean and the northernmost parts of Europe, Asia, and North America. The Arctic is cold and windy for most of the year. Scientists consider the Arctic a type of desert because

This map shows the land and water areas that make up the Arctic. The red line shows the area that has an average summer temperature of 50°F (10°C) and is the southernmost edge of the Arctic region.

CONTENTS

y

w

dr

yo

nor

mad

and t

of Eu

Ameri

and wi

Some s

Arctic a

This

dotte

50°F

4

it usually receives less than 10 inches (25.4 cm) of **precipitation** a year. Plants and animals in the Arctic have adapted for **survival** in one of the coldest, driest places on Earth. People who live in the Arctic dress for the harsh conditions.

You can see how these children (left) and the people playing basketball (above) are bundled up for protection against the subzero temperatures of the Arctic.

WHAT IS AN ECOSYSTEM?

Earth has many different forms of life. Plants, animals, and other creatures survive and flourish everywhere on our planet—from the hottest desert to the coldest mountain. Each plant and animal living in a forest, pond, desert, or jungle is part of an ecosystem.

An ecosystem is a community of living and nonliving things that functions as a single unit. Ecosystems are supported by the flow of **nutrients** throughout the community. Scientists use food webs to show this flow of nutrients. A food web is the arrangement of feeding relationships between the plants and animals in an ecosystem. All living things get the energy they need to live and grow from the nutrients they take in. A change in one part of an ecosystem often causes far-reaching changes throughout the ecosystem.

This is an example of a simple forest food web. You can follow the arrows to see how food energy is passed. The plants in a food web are called producers because they make, or produce, food. Animals are called consumers because they eat, or consume, plants or animals that eat plants.

WHAT IS A BIOME?

Biomes are large areas of land defined by their climates, geographic locations, and the types of plants and animals that live there. Biomes are large communities on Earth that have many related ecosystems. Ecosystems are grouped together in a biome and also include nonliving things, such as soil, rocks, sunlight, and water. The climate of a region affects its ecosystems. Much of the Arctic is home to tundra biomes.

The tundra biome has low **temperatures** for most of the year and little snowfall. Living conditions can be quite severe. The subzero temperatures make it a hard place for plants and animals to live. In this book, we'll look at plants and animals of the tundra and their amazing adaptations!

The map on page 9 shows the locations of Earth's major biomes. The Arctic tundra covers about 20 percent of Earth's surface. The graphic triangle shows the tundra and Earth's other major biomes in a range of temperature and moisture levels.

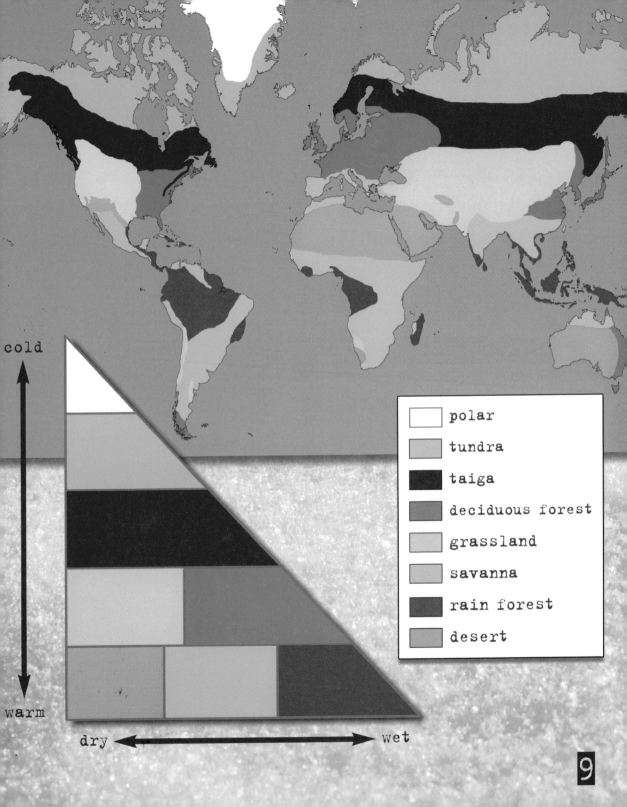

cold

warm

dry ← → wet

polar
tundra
taiga
deciduous forest
grassland
savanna
rain forest
desert

LAND OF THE MIDNIGHT SUN

The Arctic is a cold, dark place much of the year. Some areas go months without the sun rising. During other months, the sun doesn't set! The closer to the North Pole, the longer the periods of light and dark become. Even when the sun can be seen for long periods of time, the area does not get very warm because of the angle of the sun's rays.

This Arctic picture was taken around midnight in June. It shows the sun above the horizon.

The sun is below the horizon during the day in this winter picture taken in the Arctic.

At the North Pole, the sun stays above the horizon and doesn't set from about March 20 until about September 23. Because of this, the Arctic is often called the land of the midnight sun. However, the opposite is true during the long Arctic winter. At the North Pole, the sun doesn't rise above the horizon from about September 23 to about March 20!

PLANTS OF THE ARCTIC

As in all ecosystems, the plants of the Arctic are very important. Plants are called producers because they produce food for themselves using sunlight, air, and nutrients from the soil. They also produce food for animals because they pass their nutrients on to the animals that eat them.

Would you believe the Arctic is home to hundreds of plants? Arctic plants have special adaptations to help them survive the severe conditions. Most grow close to the ground. This protects them from bitter winds. The plants also spread out their roots near the surface of

These reindeer are grazing on the Canadian Arctic tundra.

The orange line on the map of the Arctic above shows the tree line. The light blue line shows the Arctic region.

the soil to get water. Arctic plants often have small, hairy leaves that help keep in heat. Mosses and short grasses grow close together and are nearly everywhere in the Arctic ecosystem. Arctic plants are even able to make their own food when they are covered with ice and snow!

Large plants, such as trees, only grow in the outer areas of the Arctic. The Arctic tree line is the northern limit of tree growth.

Summer in the Arctic is surprisingly colorful. Numerous wildflowers start to bloom as soon as the winter snow and ice begin to melt. Berries spring up around rivers, lakes, and ponds. Flowers and fruits may not last long, but they help draw many kinds of **migrating** animals in the summer.

Lichens (LY-kuhnz), an important part of almost every Arctic ecosystem, are often grouped with plants. However, they're actually a combination of an **alga** and a **fungus** that work together. The alga uses **photosynthesis** to make food for itself and

These red lichens are growing on rocks. Lichens grow very slowly—usually less than 0.04 inches (1 mm) a year! Widespread changes to the ecosystem can occur if lichens are harmed, because they take a long time to grow back.

arctic flowers

the fungus. The fungus collects nutrients and water for itself and the alga. Lichens help keep water in the ground and make it suitable for other plants. They're also an important food for many Arctic animals.

fungi

plants

Fungi, shrubs, and other small plants grow close together in the tundra soil.

ANIMALS OF THE ARCTIC

Arctic animals such as reindeer, lemmings, and squirrels are **herbivores** that eat the plentiful arctic mosses, lichens, and grasses. Arctic **carnivores** include wolves, bears, and foxes. Some animals, such as reindeer, musk oxen, and polar bears, have thick layers of fur to keep warm. Others, like the arctic hare and the arctic fox, have white fur in winter and brown fur in summer. This helps them hide from enemies.

Small herbivores called lemmings greatly affect many Arctic ecosystems. Lemming populations can grow very quickly. This harms other herbivores because large groups of lemmings can clear

This picture shows a lemming in the Arctic snow. When the lemming population is low, the number of other herbivores goes up, but the number of animals that eat lemmings goes down.

arctic fox

an entire area of plant life in a short period of time! When lemmings run out of food, they migrate in large groups to new areas.

ground squirrel

reindeer

These arctic foxes are digging in the snow looking for lemmings.

polar bear

When the weather breaks at winter's end, the snow melts to form large areas of very wet soil that are perfect insect-breeding grounds. Many insects lay eggs at the end of summer. The eggs hatch after the winter, and thick clouds of insects blanket the tundra. Some insects **hibernate** in the Arctic. Some freeze solid and thaw out in summer! Some insects that remain active year-round make a chemical that lowers the temperature at which their blood freezes! Most Arctic insects are darkly colored, which allows them to take in more of the sun's light and heat. These adaptations help insects survive in the rough Arctic climate.

butterfly

caterpillar

grasshoppper

beetle

mosquito

Migrating birds, such as snowy owls and Canada geese, travel to the Arctic every summer to eat the insects. The Arctic marshes also make good nesting grounds for birds to raise their young before leaving again for the winter.

The ptarmigan (TAHR-muh-guhn) is a bird that lives year-round in the Arctic. It eats insects, berries, and seeds. The ptarmigan is completely covered in feathers—even its bill and feet! Ptarmigans shed their feathers three times a year and grow a new coat that helps them blend in with their seasonal surroundings.

DECOMPOSERS OF THE ARCTIC

Plants and animals get their nutrients from the things around them. Plants take nutrients from the soil. Animals get nutrients from the plants and other animals they eat.

All ecosystems, including those in the Arctic, need tiny creatures called decomposers. These creatures break down, or decompose, dead plants and animals. This process puts nutrients back into the soil so they can be used again.

Decomposers in the Arctic include **bacteria**, fungi, and insect **larvae**. Bacteria are a very important part of the Arctic ecosystem because they can survive

You can see the fungus growing on this log. It will break down the log and supply the soil with nutrients from the decomposed wood.

Bacteria are breaking down this rotting tree trunk.

in frozen soil, Arctic waters, and even ice! These creatures feed on dead plants and animals, as well as the solid waste of animals. Fungi, as well as the insects that the larvae grow into, are also a food source for many Arctic animals.

This beetle larva is curled up in some decaying wood.

LIFE IN THE ARCTIC OCEAN

The Arctic Ocean makes up a large part of the Arctic region. Arctic **marine** plants and animals also have special adaptations that help them survive the subzero temperatures and very cold water.

Some animals have matter in their bodies that keeps their blood from freezing. Many, such as seals and walruses, have a thick layer of

Walruses have very long teeth called tusks. They use their tusks for fighting, cracking holes in the ice, and even pulling themselves out of the water. Did you know you can tell the age of a walrus by studying its tusks? If you cut a walrus's tusk you can count the rings you see. There is one ring for each year the walrus has lived.

fat that keeps them warm. Some have features such as long snouts that can reach down into the water, sharp claws that can capture prey, or whiskers that can feel and gather floating plants or swimming animals.

There are more than 200 kinds of ice algae living in Arctic waters. Some use light near the surface to make food. Others cling to the underside of **ice floes**, living in ice crystals, swimming through paths in the ice, or floating in the water.

These tiny plants and animals are plankton. Many Arctic marine animals depend on plankton for survival. Plankton are carried along by ocean currents.

PEOPLE OF THE ARCTIC

People have been living in the Arctic for at least 11,000 years. The Inuit live in the tundra of Canada, Greenland, and the United States. The Sami live in Sweden, Norway, Finland, and the western Russian tundra. The Khants, Nenets, Komi, and Chuckchi live in the Siberian tundra of central and eastern Russia.

Arctic peoples often have similar practices and means of survival. Living in the tundra has never been easy. While plants and animals have adapted their bodies, people have also adapted their style of living. Today, most Arctic people use modern inventions—along with ancient practices—to hunt, build, and survive in the hard, bitter conditions.

These Khant women and children are sitting outside their tents on the frozen Siberian tundra.

This traditional raised structure, built by the Sami of northern Europe, is used to store supplies.

This Inuit man rides through the very cold Arctic waters in his kayak.

The Inuit are among the most well known of the Arctic peoples. They've lived in the Arctic for thousands of years. In the past, they moved from place to place searching for food. They hunted on sea and land. In the oceans they used narrow, canoe-like boats called kayaks to hunt fish, whales, seals, and walruses and gather seaweed. On land, they hunted reindeer, polar bear, musk oxen, and birds. The Inuit not only ate the animals, they used

The Inuit sometimes use ice and snow when constructing buildings. In Canada, Inuit of the past made structures of ice and snow called igloos. Today, many Inuit still build igloos like this one while on hunting trips.

animal bones and walrus tusks to make knives and tools, animal furs to make clothing and shelter, and whale fat for fuel.

Inuit society is based on the harmonious relationship between the land, people, plants, and animals. Today, they no longer need to travel from place to place to stay alive. They live and work in settled communities. However, the Inuit honor and maintain the same values and practices of centuries ago—including tools and supplies—despite the effects of the modern world.

A CHANGING ECOSYSTEM

For many years, the Arctic was largely untouched by modern ways. Today, however, more and more people are coming to this area. People worry that new roads and buildings threaten to destroy ancient ecosystems. They are concerned that drilling for oil in some areas, such as northern Russia and northern Alaska, will destroy the balance of the ecosystem.

Recent changes in weather and temperature patterns are also changing the Arctic. **Global warming** is a gradual increase in average world temperatures. As Earth's temperature rises, the Arctic's ice is beginning to melt at a fast pace. Some people worry that these changes will harm the Arctic and believe work must start now to stop them.

This picture shows a polar bear on an ice floe in the Arctic Ocean. Polar bears may drift farther and farther out to sea as more and more ice melts due to rising Arctic temperatures. Although polar bears are good swimmers, they can drift such a long way out that swimming back becomes too tiring. Many people are concerned that polar bears will all die because of global warming.

ARCTIC ADAPTATIONS

Living things in the Arctic ecosystem have adapted well for survival. The chart below lists some of the plants and animals discussed in this book and examples of their adaptations. Now that you know about the Arctic ecosystem, you can use library books and the Internet to add more Arctic adaptations to this chart.

Arctic creature	adaptation	how it helps
moss and grass	grow close to the ground	• protects them from bitter winds • easier to get water from the soil
lichen	combination of an alga and a fungus	• each helps the other survive; the alga makes food and the fungus collects nutrients
polar bear	thick layers of fur and fat	• protect it from the cold climate
Arctic insects	size and dark coloring	• makes it easier to warm up in the sun
ptarmigan, arctic hare, arctic fox	change colors as the seasons change	• helps them blend in with their seasonal surroundings

GLOSSARY

alga (AL-guh) A plantlike living thing without roots or stem that often lives in water. The plural is algae (AL-jee).

bacteria (bak-TIHR-ee-uh) Tiny living things that cannot be seen with the eye alone.

carnivore (KAHR-nuh-vohr) An animal that eats other animals.

fungus (FUHN-guhs) A living thing that is similar to a plant but that doesn't have leaves, flowers, or green color, and doesn't make its own food. The plural is fungi (FUHN-jy).

global warming (GLOH-buhl WOHR-ming) A gradual increase in Earth's temperature. Many people think the gases released by burning fuels such as gasoline contribute to it.

herbivore (UHR-buh-vohr) An animal that eats plants.

hibernate (HY-buhr-nayt) To spend the winter in a sleeplike state.

ice floe (EYS FLOH) A large sheet of floating sea ice.

larva (LAHR-vuh) An insect in an early life stage. The plural is larvae (LAHR-vee).

marine (muh-REEN) Having to do with the sea.

migrate (MY-grayt) To move from one place to another.

nutrient (NOO-tree-unt) Food that a living thing needs to live and grow.

photosynthesis (foh-toh-SIHN-thuh-suhs) The way in which green plants make their own food from sunlight, water, and carbon dioxide.

precipitation (prih-sih-puh-TAY-shun) Moisture that falls from clouds, such as rain or snow.

survival (suhr-VY-vuhl) Continued existence.

temperature (TEHM-puhr-chur) How hot or cold something is.

INDEX